O V

I

MAKE UP YOUR MIND TO OVERCOME.

- Job is a great example of persistence in the midst of human suffering. He was stripped financially. His children were killed. His closest friends judged him guilty of some hidden sin. But, he *determined to overcome*.
- The *opinions of others will never change your character*. Ultimately and inevitably, integrity wins. *Always*.
- Whatever the price, overcoming is worth it.

WISDOM FROM THE WORD

"Though He slay me, yet will I trust in him: but I will maintain mine own ways before him."
Job 13:15

DAY 2

CHOOSE TO CONQUER.

- ❑ Many have faced adversity greater than your own. *Yet, they overcame.* Their secret was that they *chose* to conquer.
- ❑ *Stop looking for excuses to fail.* Start looking for reasons to *succeed. Overcoming is a choice.*
- ❑ The Apostle Paul received 195 lashes with a whip... beaten 3 times with rods... stoned and left for dead... shipwrecked 3 times... yet the world has never forgotten him. *He chose to conquer.*

WISDOM FROM THE WORD

"Who shall separate us from the love of Christ? shall tribulation, or distress, or persecution, or famine, or nakedness, or peril, or sword? Nay, in all these things we are more than conquerors through Him that loved us."

Romans 8:35, 37

DAY 3

CULTIVATE THE MENTALITY OF AN OVERCOMER.

- ❑ Champions *think* differently. They refuse to waste their energy and thoughts on their obstacles. Instead, they concentrate on their *goals*.
- ❑ You, too, can change your thought-life. It may take a little time, but it is well worth it.
- ❑ Fix your mind on Portraits of Victories you will experience. Now... *Move Toward Them*.

WISDOM FROM THE WORD

"Finally, brethren, whatsoever things are true, whatsoever things are honest, whatsoever things are just, whatsoever things are pure, whatsoever things are lovely, whatsoever things are of good report; if there be any virtue, and if there be any praise, think on these things."

Philippians 4:8

DAY 4

FACE YOUR PROBLEMS HONESTLY.

- ❑ Don't blame others for what *you* have chosen to do. Don't blame others for the *consequences* of your choices. *Never complain about what you permit.*
- ❑ Your life is the *result of your choices.*
- ❑ *Name your weaknesses*. Nobody else *can* do it. Nobody else *will* do it. Nobody else *should have* to do it. Your honesty will determine your victories.

WISDOM FROM THE WORD

"If we say that we have no sin,
we deceive ourselves, and the truth is
not in us. If we confess our sins,
He is faithful and just to forgive us our
sins, and to cleanse us from
all unrighteousness."

I John 1:8, 9

DAY 5

STORE UP POWER.

- ❑ The Word of God has *power*. When Jesus faced the tempter (Matthew 4), He quoted the Scriptures to *thwart* satan. *It worked*. Jesus won.
- ❑ Discipline yourself for the next 30 days to read one chapter a day. Begin with the book of Acts.
- ❑ It is the Power-Book of the Bible. *Store it up* within you. Prayer produces *joy*. The Word produces *power*. Do both *daily*. *Nothing will ever dominate your life unless it happens daily*.

WISDOM FROM THE WORD

"For the word of God is quick, and powerful, and sharper than any twoedged sword, piercing even to the dividing asunder of soul and spirit, and of the joints and marrow, and is a discerner of the thoughts and intents of the heart."

Hebrews 4:12

DAY 6

LEARN THE ART OF ATTACK.

- ❑ Overcomers are *not* passive. They *pursue*. They cannot tolerate enslavement.
- ❑ *What you fail to master will eventually master you*. It may be anger, an addiction or an attitude.
- ❑ *Target* your enemy. *God loves a fighter*. Paul attacked tradition. Jesus attacked sickness and disease. Go ahead... learn the joy of attack.

WISDOM FROM THE WORD

"Blessed be the Lord my strength, which teacheth my hands to war, and my fingers to fight."
Psalms 144:1

DAY 7

KNOW YOUR OPPONENT.

- ❑ Satan is your *real* adversary. He is a *fallen* angel, dispelled from heaven by a righteous God.
- ❑ His methods are predictable. He *incites* the violent nature of men against you. He *inflames* the normal passions of man into perversion. He *introduces* thoughts that could ultimately destroy you.
- ❑ He reacts to the *spoken* Word of God. He is easily demoralized with the *Weapon of Praise.* He flees when you *resist* him.

WISDOM FROM THE WORD

"For we wrestle not against flesh and blood, but against principalities, against powers, against the rulers of the darkness of this world, against spiritual wickedness in high places."

Ephesians 6:12

DAY 8

UNLEASH THE HOLY SPIRIT WITHIN YOU.

- ❑ The Holy Spirit is a *Person*. A *Teacher*. A *Companion*. He is the *Presence* and the *Power* of God.
- ❑ Before The Experience, Peter was cowardly, denying Jesus Christ. *After* The Experience, he won thousands to Christ instead.
- ❑ *Obey* the voice of the Holy Spirit within you...*hourly*. Don't take His instructions lightly. *Each instruction is linked to an event in your future.*

WISDOM FROM THE WORD

"But ye shall receive power, after that the Holy Ghost is come upon you: and ye shall be witnesses unto me both in Jerusalem, and in all Judea, and in Samaria, and unto the uttermost part of the earth."

Acts 1:8

DAY 9

LISTEN TO PAIN.

- ❑ Pain is *discomfort created by disorder*. It is *not* really an enemy. It is a *signal, a memo,* a *messenger* telling you an enemy exists.
- ❑ When you were a child, you may have touched a hot iron, It hurt! Pain made you jerk your hand away... *make changes...* to *protect* yourself from injury.
- ❑ If things are going wrong in your life, take it seriously. *Pain talks*. Initiate any *change* that may be necessary.

WISDOM FROM THE WORD

"...Weeping may endure for a night, but joy cometh in the morning"
Psalms 30:5b

DAY 10

USE THE WEAPON OF PRAISE.

- ❑ King Saul was often tormented by evil spirits. When this happened, he called for David, the Psalmist and shepherd boy, to play the harp. The evil spirits always departed.
- ❑ *Praise and worship are dreaded weapons in hell.* Demon powers are demoralized by it.
- ❑ *Don't neglect this weapon.* It is too powerful to ignore. As you lift your hands in worship and praise, you will literally *purge the atmosphere* of demonic activity.

WISDOM FROM THE WORD

"And it came to pass, when the evil spirit from God was upon Saul, that David took an harp, and played with his hand: so Saul was refreshed, and was well, and the evil spirit departed from him."

I Samuel 16:23

DAY 11

RECOGNIZE YOUR DELIVERER.

- ❑ God *assigns* Deliverers. Moses was *assigned* to lead the Israelites out of Egypt. Elijah was *sent* to the widow of Zarephath to help her use her faith for provision.
- ❑ If you are sick, *look* for the man of God who believes in *healing*. If you are having financial problems, *look* for the man of God who *believes in prosperity*.
- ❑ *No one fails alone*. If you fail, it will be because you *chose to ignore those God assigned to help you*.

WISDOM FROM THE WORD

"O Jerusalem, Jerusalem, thou that killest the prophets, and stonest them which are sent unto thee, how often would I have gathered thy children together, even as a hen gathereth her chickens under her wings, and ye would not! Behold, your house is left unto you desolate.." Matthew 23:37, 38

DAY 12

REACH FOR HELP.

- ❑ *Reaching out for help is not a sign of weakness*. So, do it. Only a fool ignores a lifejacket when he is drowning.
- ❑ *Overcomers don't do it alone*. They conquer their pride. They reject the *trap of isolation*. They *reach*. They *know* the inevitable reward of reaching.
- ❑ *Turn to God*. Honor those who are qualified to help you. *Your future depends on it*.

WISDOM FROM THE WORD

"When thou art in tribulation, and all these things are come upon thee, even in the latter days, if thou turn to the Lord thy God, and shalt be obedient unto his voice; (For the Lord thy God is a merciful God;) he will not forsake thee, neither destroy thee, nor forget the covenant of thy fathers which he swore unto them."

Deuteronomy 4:30, 31

DAY 13

TALK LIKE A VICTOR NOT A VICTIM.

- ❑ Your words are *signals... scents*. They can be like the fragrance of a rose or the odor of a skunk. They can *attract or repel*.
- ❑ *Don't talk like a "victim."* It invites pity, but not partnership. Even in the animal kingdom the wounded are attacked, not assisted.
- ❑ Your words are continually *educating* others around you. Let them create a portrait of enthusiasm and faith.

WISDOM FROM THE WORD

"Death and life are in the power of the tongue: and they that love it shall eat the fruit thereof."
Proverbs 18:21

DAY 14

ENDURE. ENDURE. ENDURE.

- ❑ *Overcoming involves more than one battle.* The man who *refuses* to quit... always wins. *Always!*
- ❑ The mysterious, invisible quality of Champions is *endurance*. They refuse to run from a fight. They *insist* on one more round.
- ❑ *Don't ever consider quitting*. Get up and try again. And again! And *again*!! Hell fears a fighter.

WISDOM FROM THE WORD

"Blessed is the man that endureth temptation: for when He is tried, He shall receive the crown of life, which the Lord hath promised to them that love Him."

James 1:12

DAY 15

DON'T NEGLECT YOUR SPIRITUAL ARMOR.

- ❑ It is *invisible*. It is *overlooked*. Yet, like air, it still exists. As a soldier in the army of God, *you must put on your spiritual armor* during your morning prayer time.
- ❑ Pray this prayer: "Father, I wrap your *Truth* around my loins. I wear the breastplate of your *Righteousness*. My feet walk in your Peace. I take the *Shield of Faith*. I wear the helmet of *Salvation*. Your *Word* will be the weapon in my mouth today, the *Sword of the Spirit*. I wear the protection of your armor and nothing shall harm me in any way today."
- ❑ Believe me, this armor, though invisible to *you*, is highly apparent to satan, your enemy. *Put it on.*

WISDOM FROM THE WORD

"Put on the whole armour of God, that ye may be able to stand against the wiles of the devil." Ephesians 6:11

DAY 16

USE YOUR PRAYER LANGUAGE.

- ❑ Millions are discovering the remarkable secret of praying in the Spirit... *praying in an unknown language*. The Apostle Paul did it. You can, too.
- ❑ Become *uninhibited* in your prayer life. Permit the Heavenly language to flow out of you toward the Father.
- ❑ Talk to God about this supernatural experience. It is one of the most effective tools in the life of an Overcomer. *Use. it*.

WISDOM FROM THE WORD

"Likewise the Spirit also helpeth our infirmities: for we know not what we should pray for as we ought: but the Spirit itself maketh intercession for us with groanings which cannot be uttered. And he that searcheth the hearts knoweth what is the mind of the Spirit, because he maketh intercession for the saints according to the will of God." Romans 8:26, 27

"But ye, beloved, building up yourselves on your most holy faith, praying in the Holy Ghost." Jude 20

DAY 17

EXPECT SUPERNATURAL INTERVENTION.

- ❑ Elisha and his servant were surrounded by Syrian soldiers. The servant, trembling with fear, cried, "Alas my master! How shall we do?"
- ❑ Elisha answered, "Fear not: for they that be with us are more than they that be with them." The servant's eyes were opened and he saw the invisible army of angels *supernaturally assigned* to protect them.
- ❑ *Expect the Supernatural*. Angels are assigned to you. Never underestimate the attentiveness of you Father. *Nothing is ever as bad as it first appears.*

WISDOM FROM THE WORD

"He giveth power to the faint; and to them that have no might he increaseth strength."
Isaiah 40:29

"And Elisha prayed, and said, Lord, I pray thee, open his eyes, that he may see. And the Lord opened the eyes of the young man; and he saw: and, behold, the mountain was full of horses and chariots of fire round about Elisha." II Kings 6:17

DAY 18

REFUSE TO FEAR.

- ❑ *Fear attracts attack.* Even animals have been known to attack humans when they have sensed fear.
- ❑ Fear is the *feeling of anticipated loss.* It may be loss of reputation, property, love, health or life.
- ❑ *Loss is not fatal.* First, everything you presently possess was given to you by God. Second, whatever you have given back to God cannot be stolen by men. Third, anything man has ever taken from you, God has promised to restore.

WISDOM FROM THE WORD

"And I will restore to you the years that the locust hath eaten, the cankerworm, and the caterpillar, and the palmerworm, my great army which I sent among you."

Joel 2:25

"For God hath not given us the spirit of fear; but of power, and of love, and of a sound mind."

II Timothy 1:7

DAY 19

RISK EVERYTHING TO BE AN OVERCOMER.

- ❑ *Overcomers are the Rewarded.* In fact, they are the *only* ones who are rewarded through eternity.
- ❑ Even the Apostle Paul counted everything as loss *except* his position with Christ. *Each victory authorizes God to promote you.*
- ❑ In the World System, *birth* may decide rank. In the Kingdom System, *battle* decides rank. *Every satanic attack upon you is simply another opportunity for promotion.*

WISDOM FROM THE WORD

"I have fought a good fight, I have finished my course, I have kept the faith: Henceforth there is laid up for me a crown of righteousness, which the Lord, the righteous judge, shall give me at that day: and not to me only, but unto all them also that love his appearing."
II Timothy 4:7, 8

DAY 20

GROW YOUR FAITH.

- ❑ *Everything begins small.* The oak tree began with an acorn. The skyscraper began with a brick.
- ❑ Even weightlifters started their careers with just a few pounds. Little by little, they birthed new levels of strength and power.
- ❑ *Water the Seeds of Faith* in your heart. Give them a chance to grow. *You are just a portion of what you will be tomorrow.*

WISDOM FROM THE WORD

"For who hath despised the day of small things?..."
Zechariah 4:10a

"Though thy beginning was small, yet thy latter end should greatly increase."
Job 8:7

DAY 21

WAKE UP THE SEED OF GOD WITHIN YOU.

- ❑ *You are the offspring of a perfect God.* This explains your appetite for order, excellence and perfection.
- ❑ *You are the offspring of a warring God.* This explains your warfare with satan and evil.
- ❑ *You are the offspring of an overcoming God.* So, wake up the dormant seed within you. Release His Holy Spirit to work through you today.

WISDOM FROM THE WORD

"Ye are of God, little children, and have overcome them: because greater is He that is in you, than he that is in the world."

I John 4:4

DAY 22

RUN TO THE REFUGE.

- ❑ Cities of refuge existed in Old Testament times. If a man was accused of a crime, he could run into a city of refuge and was guaranteed protection by law.
- ❑ You, too, have a Place of Refuge. When satan the accuser, brings accusations against your life, *run to God*.
- ❑ God responds to *reachers. Stop looking at where you have been, and start looking at where you can be.* Run to the Refuge. Do it today.

WISDOM FROM THE WORD

"For thou hast been a strength to the poor, a strength to the needy in his distress, a refuge from the storm, a shadow from the heat, when the blast of the terrible ones is as a storm against the wall."
Isaiah 25:4

DAY 23

SOW A BATTLE-SEED.

- ❑ Your Seed is anything you do that helps another. It may be information, encouragement, or even finances. Whatever it is, *Your Seed Is Always Your Door Out Of Trouble.*
- ❑ Job sowed a prayer of deliverance for his three friends. *Then*, God turned Job's captivity around. David stopped a tragedy by offering a special offering to the Lord.
- ❑ *Your contribution to someone in trouble always unlocks God's contribution back into your life.*

WISDOM FROM THE WORD

"And David built there an altar unto the Lord, and offered burnt offerings and peace offerings. So the Lord was intreated for the land, and the plague was stayed from Israel." II Samuel 24:25

"Give, and it shall be given unto you; good measure, pressed down, and shaken together, and running over, shall men give into your bosom. For with the same measure that ye mete withal it shall be measured to you again." Luke 6:38

DAY 24

KEEP YOUR FOCUS.

- ❑ The Secret of Success is *concentration*. The Secret of Failure is *broken focus*.
- ❑ The forbidden fruit *distracted* Adam and Eve. Delilah *distracted* Samson. *Whatever takes your mind away from God's assignment is an instrument of Hell.*
- ❑ Examine your life... "Honestly." Disconnect from every distraction. *Fix your focus.* Don't let satan ever get a foot inside your door. *You are too close to Victory to lose out now.*

WISDOM FROM THE WORD

"Only be thou strong and very courageous, that thou mayest observe to do according to all the law, which Moses my servant commanded thee: turn not from it to the right hand or to the left, that thou mayest prosper whithersoever thou goest."

Joshua 1:7

DAY 25

REMEMBER THE TREE OF LIFE.

- ❑ *Overcomers are ultimately rewarded.* Even the Apostle Paul anticipated a crown of righteousness.
- ❑ Don't forfeit Heaven for one weak moment. Too much is at stake.
- ❑ *Heaven is waiting.* A parade of celebration is about to begin. *Keep your eyes on paradise.* The grand-stands of Heaven are full of champions who have gone on before you. REMEMBER!

WISDOM FROM THE WORD

"He that hath an ear, let him hear what the Spirit saith unto the churches; To him that overcometh will I give to eat of the tree of life, which is in the midst of the paradise of God."

Revelation 2:7

DAY 26

REMEMBER THE CROWN OF LIFE.

- ❑ *Overcoming is not a small thing to God.* He celebrates faithfulness. Forever.
- ❑ Don't give in to satan today. *In anything.* You are too close to your Rewards.
- ❑ A moment of pain is worth an eternity of gain. *Go for the Crown!*

WISDOM FROM THE WORD

"...Be thou faithful unto death, and I will give thee a crown of life... He that overcometh shall not be hurt of the second death."
Revelation 2:10b, 11b

DAY 27

REMEMBER THE WHITE STONE.

- ❑ You may be sorely tempted today. Satan may inflame every appetite of your flesh. *Stay strong.*
- ❑ You are a Trophy of the grace of God. Hell is incensed over your loyalty to God.
- ❑ *Your Reward Ceremony is closer than you realize.* Hidden manna... a white stone... and your new Name. Your happiness has just begun. *You are too close to Home to turn back now.*

WISDOM FROM THE WORD

"He that hath an ear, let him hear what the Spirit saith unto the churches; To him that overcometh will I give to eat of the hidden manna, and will give him a white stone, and in the stone a new name written, which no man knoweth saving he that receiveth it."

Revelation 2:17

DAY
28

REMEMBER YOUR RULERSHIP.

- ❑ *Overcomers are always on God's mind.* He has declared that He will turn the nations of the earth over to Overcomers.
- ❑ Don't weaken in The Battle Of Life today. *You are too close to promotion.* Every general knows that rulership is worth the price of discipline. Short-term pain for long-term gain.
- ❑ Each victory is a step toward the throne. A giant step. *You are closer than you have ever been to the Palace. START ACTING LIKE ROYALTY.*

WISDOM FROM THE WORD

"And he that overcometh, and keepeth my works unto the end, to him will I give power over the nations: And he shall rule them with a rod of iron; as the vessels of a potter shall they be broken to shivers: even as I received of my Father. And I will give him the morning star."

Revelation 2:26-28